REBORN
at **36**

REBORN
at **36**

PEDRO LEBRON

XULON PRESS

Xulon Press
2301 Lucien Way #415
Maitland, FL 32751
407.339.4217
www.xulonpress.com

Printed in the United States of America.

ISBN-13: 978-1-6305-0375-8

TABLE OF CONTENTS

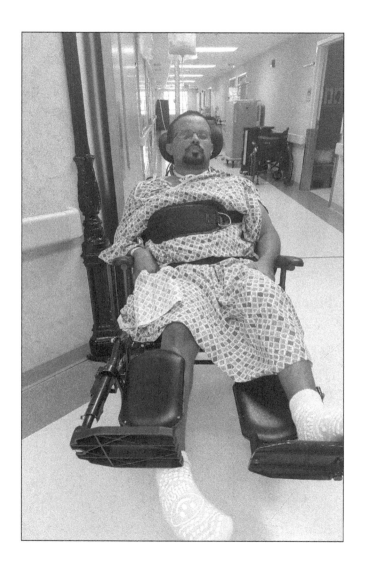

REBORN

When I say I was reborn at thirty-six, I mean that when I was thirty-six, I returned to a state in which I had to be cared for like a baby. I had to be fed, wear diapers, and everything else. This all came about because I had a life-changing accident. I literally died and came back to life. I was reborn. I feel I need to share my story. Maybe it will do somebody some good in the long run. Maybe it will motivate someone to keep living and let them know that life itself is truly a gift. Maybe I just need to share.

Now, I thought of sharing my story, and I thought about how I would do that. But it wasn't until my fourteen-year-old son told me I should do it that I really had the desire to move forward and put the story into words. My son, Isaiah, is incredible, and we'll definitely talk more about him and my daughter and how important their roles in all of this have been. They're very important to me and have played significant roles in this entire story. Nobody had to write their scripts. They knew exactly what to do and when. I feel truly blessed. My kids are wonderful. They are so full of love and care for their old man that it's extremely difficult to put into words.

I did some pretty cool things in my first short life. I imitated Elvis in the halftime show of a national college football game. I danced salsa professionally on international TV. I definitely did some bad things too. Growing up, you experience bad times and good times. I definitely gave my mom some headaches growing up, but that's later in the story.

Now, before I start, I want to let you know that this book does not have chapters. I refuse to put my life into numbers. My life has not been numbers but stages, I would say. Therefore, I'm going to name them according to how they apply to the story. For example, this first stage of my life is Puerto Rico.

PUERTO RICO

I lived in Puerto Rico a total of eight years. It was almost nine, but I wasn't quite born there. But the Boricua pride is there as if I had been. My father was in the army when I was born; therefore, I was born in Worchester, MA, according to my mother. (I'll definitely talk more about her later. She's a big and important part of this story. In my opinion, the most important person in my life has definitely been Mom.) Anyway, I lived there until I was one, and then I moved to Puerto Rico. It's my understanding that I was there from one to nine years old before moving to the US mainland. This is very important again, and will also be discussed more later.

My years in Puerto Rico were by far some of the best in my life. Growing up with all my cousins definitely had a big impact on my life. I played with them day in and day out. We grew up in a very small town called Gurabo. Our neighborhood was built half on a mountain and half down below. We used to take our bikes to the top of the hill and ride all the way down. There are many stories to write about that hill. There were a lot of bumps and bruises for all of us, but there was a lot of fun too. We used to live across the street from a river, so we went fishing a lot. Fish would not go to waste, of course. We would bring them home for a late lunch or dinner. When you're that poor, there are no fishing poles. We used a can with fishing line wrapped around it and a fish hook on the end of the line. We put rocks inside the can so we would know when a fish was on the line. Not for nothing, but we were pretty good fisherman. We definitely caught more than one would expect. We would only go for one or two hours at the most, but we'd come home with four or five fish each to eat. They were mostly catfish, but when you're hungry, who the heck cares what kind of fish they are?

Between all the cousins and neighborhood friends, there were enough of us to have two baseball teams. We played baseball a lot. I had my first taste of fame in baseball, but it definitely wasn't the last. This was just a taste of fame. I was more like Mr. Popular. My other experiences with fame involve TV shows, international channels, and lots of fans. We will definitely dive into that later on.

My mom signed me up for the local baseball team. At first, my position was catcher. One day, we were playing another local team, and we were getting our asses whipped. Our pitcher kept giving up runs. Our guys were upset and bored with the game by then. So, I begged and begged the coach to let me pitch. I don't know why, I just thought I could do a better job than this guy. I had absolutely no reason to think I could do better. I had never pitched before, except in neighborhood games with my cousins. I figured this guy sucked so bad, there was no way I could do worse.

The coach said, "What the heck? What else do we have to lose?"

So he let me pitch, and my gosh. Not to blow my own horn, but I became the man. What a pitcher! The other team was not able to score again. I had the crowd going crazy. For some reason, I was throwing strike after strike. It was really cool. I kept saluting the crowd as I was pitching. I thought I was famous.

Even the coach had to tell me to knock it off. "Okay, Mr. Popular, stop waiving at the crowd, and stay focused."

The crowd eventually learned my name. They kept cheering it. My beautiful mom was in the crowd, so I figured they learned my name from her. That game completely turned around. We won that game—and a lot more for the rest of the season. My coach kept me as the pitcher. At the end of the year, I got a medal with an inscription that read Best Pitcher in the League. I still own it to this day.

I was very young then, so I only have a few selective memories from there. You know how it is when you grow up playing with other kids day in and day out. There are going to be good days and bad days—fighting days. We used to fight each other as well as strangers. I was a pretty confident youngster. I definitely was not one to just slink away and not defend myself. I don't know why I always remember this, but I do. My older cousin and I must have been in the fourth grade. He's a year older, so I must have been in third grade.

One day, I came across my cousin fighting with this other kid, who must have been into karate or something. He was kicking and jumping across the hallway and having his way with my cousin. Well, I obviously was not just going to sit there and let my cousin get beat up, so I jumped in to defend him. I didn't know anything about karate or any martial arts, but dammit, I could throw a punch. He wasn't going to beat my cousin. Now he had to fight me. I got in there and started swinging, and my cousin didn't get hit any more. I just kept swinging until there was no more fight.

I got a lot of credit from the other kids for defending my cousin. I'm not saying I was Mr. Hero because I beat up the kid. What I'm saying is that I stopped my cousin from getting beat up, and I defended both of us very well. The karate kid never messed with us again.

I had good times and bad times in Puerto Rico. One of the bad times was when Hurricane Hugo hit Puerto Rico in late 1989. It came into the island as a category three. That was a devastating storm. My mom's house was made out of blocks and cement, like most houses on the island, so we felt pretty safe there. My mom and dad were divorce by then, so it was just my mom, my sisters, and I. My mom's father, Porfirio, lived around the way. That was my mom's only family on the island. Other family members who lived in the neighborhood—my cousins, other grandfather and grandmother, and aunts—were part of my father's family. My mom's father would come over often. He was a good man and another significant part of my life. During the hurricane, he was over at our house. So it was him, my mother, my two sisters, and I. We hunkered down while the storm was passing by. The winds were over 111 miles per hour. Really strong. I remember looking out the window—when mom wasn't watching, of course—and seeing the neighbors' wood house being torn apart. It was basically flying away. One of our neighbors had a horse, and his dumb ass tied the horse to a tree, thinking he would be okay. (Sorry, neighbor, if your reading this book.) Well, the storm picked up and pulled the poor horse so bad that it was strangled by its harness. We got to go outside when the eye of the storm was passing through. For those of you who have never been in a hurricane, inside the eye of the storm, it's actually quiet and calm. The winds and the chaos stop for that short period of time while the eye is passing over. It was the coolest sky I've ever seen in my life. The colors, the way the clouds were moving, and just the way it felt being there were amazing. It was like sitting right next to the monster before it attacked. Crazy!

Now, I know a hurricane is not cool. I know it's a natural disaster, and I know many people have lost their lives in such storms. My heart and my prayers go out to the families who've lost love ones in similar circumstances.

The hurricane must have went on for a few hours, but it felt like an eternity. Our house and a few others got flooded, but, thank God, no one in our neighborhood was seriously hurt. But there were more horrifying stories from other parts of the island.

I also went to the beach a lot with my father's family. I would see them on a daily basis. We used to live in the same neighborhood. My grandfather Porfirio came in about once a week to see Mom. Since he was retired, I would spend the weekend with him as many times as I was allowed. He was a really good man, a retired sergeant from the army. Out of the three of us (my two sisters and I), I was the one that spent lots of time with Porfirio. After Hugo passed, I went with him and his friend Vicente to the river to take a bath. As you can imagine, we had no water at home.

One of my worst memories, and the only truly bad memory from my time in Puerto Rico is this. My grandfather Porfirio had heart problems. I remember Mom talking about a previous heart attack he'd endure before I was born. I remember her yelling at him when he would eat red meat.

One night, in the middle of the night, my mom came into the bedroom I shared with my sisters. She was frantic. She woke us up saying, "It's Dad. It's Dad." Apparently, he'd gone to the bathroom in the middle of the night, and he'd had a heart attack. My mom had tried to open the door, but she couldn't because he was laying on the floor next to the door. We all went crazy, my older sister and I were trying to help Mom open the bathroom door as much as we could. I was nine years old at the time. My older sister is three years older than me, and my younger sister is five years younger. So this was a very traumatic moment for Mom and us. I don't remember much after that. I don't really want to either, but unfortunately, he was gone. My grandfather, a good friend, was dead.

As a retired army man, he had a military service and funeral. It was very nice and memorable for me. He's buried in a very nice military cemetery in Puerto Rico. I get upset when I think about it, because I've been to Puerto Rico so many times after, and not once have I thought of going to visit him.

My mom was devastated. He was the only family she had nearby. Her only remaining family member, aside from her children, was her younger sister in California. She no longer had any reason to stay in Puerto Rico. As previously stated, she and my dad were divorced, and we lived in a neighborhood near his family. Now the only family member she had on the island was gone, so she no longer had a reason to stay in Puerto Rico. She decided to connect with her only family member, in California, her younger sister, my aunt. Looking back at it now, the best decision my mother made was to move to California. I believe my sisters and I are the people we are today because of California. It's unfortunate that it took my grandfather's tragedy to get us there, but my years in California were some of the best of my life. I still miss it to this day.

CALIFORNIA

California, the Golden State, and in my story, the place where I spent my golden years. Like any mother would do, mine sought the best thing for us. After my grandfather tragically died, it was time for a new beginning. When we left Puerto Rico, we were very excited about the new place. To this day, moving to a place, a new state, with a new language, has been one of the hardest things I've done in my life. Not only did I not have cousins or friends, but I also couldn't communicate with anyone. They should have ESL classes on the plane or something, to get you prepared and somewhat familiar with the language.

We lived in a very small apartment complex when we got there. Funny how things are. There was a boy living in the same complex around my age that was mute. It wasn't funny that the boy was mute, of course. It was just funny that a mute boy turned out to be my first friend when I couldn't speak the language of our new home. His name was Carlos. He used to come to my house and ask for me with a hand gesture indicating my height. I was always short. I'm short still—five four, to be exact. But that's what he would do when my mom opened the door. He put his hand down to my height so that my mom new he was looking for me. I ran into him years later at one of the many junior highs I attended during my more active years. I'll explain what I mean by more active years later on. If my mom were here, she'd definitely have something to say about that. Carlos, if by any chance you're reading this, wherever you are, hello, friend. I hope you and family are doing well.

I lived in California a total of ten years, from 1990 to 2000, to be exact. We moved almost every single year while we were there. It wasn't for anything bad. My mom was just trying to improve our status and give us a better life.

That's where I had my first taste of real fame, unlike the time I was Mr. Popular in baseball. When I was eleven, unlike most kids that age, one of the things I liked to do to pass time was listen to Elvis Presley and impersonate him in my room. My mom's boyfriend at the time, Marcos, had a guitar, so I used to use that when imitating him. I don't remember the first time I heard Elvis. I do remember the first time I saw him on TV. It was on the *Ed Sullivan Show*. Elvis was singing "Blue Suede Shoes." It was around 1956. I definitely liked his performance a lot. I used to listen to him all the time.

One day in 1991, my mother, sisters, and I went to the mall. It must have been January at the time, because there was an Elvis show at the mall. His birthday is on January 8, and they normally do shows and/or performances around that time. Anyway, at the show, there was a clipboard with a message on it that said they were looking for Elvis impersonators and to sign the page if interested. Of course, I signed.

They called me around December of 1991. There was a big event scheduled for January 1992 at Stanford University, in Stanford, California. I was invited to imitate Elvis in the halftime show at the Shrines game. By the way, I might be a little off on my dates, but this did happen around this time. For those of you not familiar, it's my understanding, that the Shrines game is where they select the best college football players from the east and the west, and they form two teams to play against each other. At the show, there would be another dozen or so Elvis impersonators. The Flying Elvises were also there and scheduled to parachute into the stadium as we danced on the field. It was a very big show. Thousands of football and Elvis fans were in attendance, and even more saw it on TV. The game was televised nationwide.

Imagine me giving the news to my mother. "Hey, Mom, we have to get an Elvis costume, and you have to take me to Stanford to imitate Elvis on TV."

"Who? What? Where?" said my mom. " What the heck are you talking about?" Actually, my mother was by far the coolest mother ever. She had a lot of confidence in us/me. She went along with it; she went along with me. We somehow somewhere found the costume, and we rented it. Finding it in my size was a miracle. It was a little black jumpsuit like the ones he used to wear.

Being a parent myself, I believe that was one of the best qualities my mom had. She showed a lot of trust and respect for us. She listen to us and valued our opinions and made sure we knew she was listening. I'm definitely practicing some of the same habits with my children. I'm not saying my mom was perfect, because I was not the perfect son. But her willingness to help me with things like this definitely made a difference in the way I viewed my mother and the relationship I had with her. I practice what I learned from her, and it has definitely made a difference in the relationship I have with my children. I have a boy, Isaiah, who's getting into that very famous teenage stage. So I'm more than willing to try better ways to connect with him.

To prepare for the event, we all met on a remote field. They took us through the plan, and we got ready. We were scheduled to walk out onto the field at halftime, salute, and dance. At the same time, the Flying Elvises would parachute in. By the way, the Flying Elvises were featured in a movie that had premiered around at that time with Nicholas Cage, *Leaving Las Vegas*. Thank God, everything went as planned. It was a great show, a great performance, and apparently a great sky dive. Everything went lovely, and it was a super cool day. I'm still trying to track down a copy of what aired on TV that day for my records.

I must have done something good that day because, believe it or not, out of all the impersonators, I was the only one invited to perform, as Elvis of course, at the Hewlett-Packard corporate office. If I remember correctly, it was nearby in Palo Alto, CA, which is right next to Stanford. They were having some kind of employee appreciation event outside in the parking lot, and I don't know why they wanted an Elvis-related performance, but they wanted me to perform. They had a stage and sound system set up outside just for my performance. I felt like I was famous. A large crowd was also waiting for my performance.

I'm sharing these stories with you to allow you to get a little more familiar with me. This way you can know a little more about me as a person before I had my life-changing accident and experience. Then maybe you can make a better decision as to why you believe that happen to me. I've made my decision. A lot of people believe things happen to you for a reason. I believe I know why this happen to me. Maybe we agree maybe we don't. We will see as we get closer. Meanwhile, I will continue to hopefully not bore you with my stories and/or events.

After my performance for HP, I fell in love, or I lost for the first time. I will let you decide which. My older sister brought home what would soon turn out to be her best friend. She was this gorgeous, 100 percent blonde Italian girl. I saw her and fell in love for the very first time. I had to make her my girlfriend. She was my older sisters friend, so she was older than me as well. I was twelve at the time; she was fifteen. I know what you're thinking. Twelve years old? Please! I had to learn to wipe my butt first before falling in love.

I invited her for a day out, and to my surprise she accepted. Yes, I was surprised. It's not every day you go after an older woman, especially at that age. I took the bus for two hours in order to spend the day with her. I picked her up, and we went to a nearby park. She was a very active girl. She was on her high school swim team. Therefore, she was a very good sport. We ended up playing basketball at the park. It was not what I would normally plan on a date with a girl, especially at that age, but what the heck. It was a great day. We had a great time. And the day had an even better ending.

At the end of the day, we were walking back to the bus stop so I could catch the bus home. Well,

I got brave. I asked her for a kiss. She thought about it hard and was cautious, but she did it. She kissed me. I remember being on the bus on the way home and celebrating. I was yelling out loud, "Yes!" I was very happy she kissed me.

A short time after that, I asked her to be my girlfriend, and she accepted. We were together as boyfriend and girlfriend for eight months or so. To this day, she's still my sister's best friend, and she and I remain friends as well. She's a very good and cool friend. She made me promise that if I shared this story, I would not use names. Since she was this really hot blond Italian girl, I called her Blondie. So, Blondie, I kept my promise—no names. I love you still. Be good!

After Blondie, my life took a turn for the worse. I got in a lot of trouble and gave my poor mother lots of headaches. Here come those more active years I was talking about. I started doing things you can't even imagine. There were a couple of things I always think about specifically. Later, I will elaborate and tell you why I think it is important to mention these two specific events. I did a lot of stupid things, but that is another story. I am not sure how to start this story but here it goes.

When I was around fifteen, I got into many bad things, including selling drugs. One guy I sold drugs to was a guy that worked as a salesman at a nearby car dealership. He fell into debt with me, and the only way for him to pay his debt, I guess, was to give me the keys to a lockbox at the dealership. The lockbox is a small box that some large dealerships use in order to store the keys to all the cars. It goes on the window of each car. This way, instead of each salesman holding the keys to a hundred different cars, they only carried one key—to the lockbox. When showing a vehicle for sale, with access to the lockbox, they have access to the keys to each car they want to show. Well, he gave me the keys, and I came up with a plan to steal one of the vehicles. At the time, I also had another lady customer that worked at the DMV. The plan was to steal the vehicle and, through the DMV lady, get it registered and sell it. Now that I think about it, the plan wouldn't have worked for many reasons, but that was the plan.

One day, I went to the dealership early in the morning, around five thirty. I was very well dressed in a button-down shirt and slacks. I was so well dressed that from looking at me, there was no way anyone would think I was there to do something I was not supposed to. In case anybody saw me, as far as they were concerned, I was just a salesman going to work early. The dealership had a parking lot in the rear with their back-up inventory. I looked around and was able to pick the car I wanted. It ended up being a 1996 Rodeo Isuzu.

I'm not proud to say this, but I stole that vehicle. I had my girl at the DMV assign me a temporary tag, and I drove the vehicle for weeks. Everything was fine and dandy, until my mom's boyfriend's brother came into the picture. He was not a good person—a real piece of work. He got jealous of my cricket success at the time, so he ratted me out for all the bad reasons. He told the cops when I was leaving the house. As I was driving down the street, I noticed the police on the side of the road looking at every vehicle except mine when I passed by. So I somehow knew they were there for me.

They pulled me over, and after a brief foot chase, I went to jail that evening. I was in the interrogation room, and I figured I was screwed, that I'd be going to jail for a long time. I came clean. I told the cops everything, including where I got the vehicle, how I got it, and what I planned to do with it. For some reason, they never asked about the tag, so I never said anything about it. I was in it all by myself, and I let them know that.

Here goes the crazy part. I couldn't even make this up if I wanted to. The cops contacted the dealership. The staff told the cops they weren't missing a car and had nothing to report stolen. How could I be charged for something stolen if it hasn't been stolen from anywhere? What I believe happened was that since I took the vehicle from the back parking lot, where they receive their shipments, that vehicle was not in their inventory yet. Basically, they were not yet aware they were missing one. Believe it or not, after I'd spent hours in the interrogation room, the cops had to let me go. They even took me home. On the way home, because I was in the interrogation room for hours, I was hungry. I told the police officer I was hungry, and being the nice man that he was, he offered me McDonalds. And, of course, I accepted. Imagine this for a moment. I was handcuffed in the back of the car, and the police officer goes through the drive-through.

The girl behind the window asked, "How can I help you?"

The officer looked back at me and asked what I wanted. Imagine the girl's face. I bet she'd never had an officer take a criminal through the drive-through and ask him what he wanted. Hilarious, now that I think about it. Incredible!

Now I have to say this, and when I say have to, I don't mean someone is telling me to do it. This is from the bottom of my heart. To all the police officers out there. I just want to say that

I am a grown man now, and I have the utmost respect for what you do and your dedication. I would never think of doing something even close to this again. I even have friends now that are officers, and I personally know your job is not easy. I admire what you guys do. Thank you for your service. I'm truly sorry about the story, but I have to tell the truth, and unfortunately, this is it.

When I got home, my mother was somewhat clueless about what had happened. She didn't know the level of what I'd done or what had really happen. Her only reaction was, "How that hell do you get in these problems, and even more, how the hell do you get out of them?"

I really didn't have an answer to that at the time. I was a little clueless myself as to what had really happened. The best part of the story involves my mom's boyfriend's brother. He lived with us at the time. Imagine his face when he came home and saw me laying in front of the TV, watching TV like nothing. He didn't say much, but his face said it all.

The cops told me somebody told them when I was leaving from the house. The only person home at the time, and the only one that knew when I was leaving, was him. Without meaning to, of course, the cops had ratted him out. I'm sorry, but I have to also say this. It's funny how things are.

Apparently, he was pulled over a short time after, and because he had drugs in the car or something similar, he went to jail for a couple of years. He wasn't as lucky as I was. I'm a firm believer in karma. You get what you dish out.

I'm only sharing these story with you because I think they're relevant, and I will explain later on how and why I think that is.

There's another story similar to the one about the car. It was me being a lot dumber but similar. I borrowed a vehicle from one of my friends at school. I should have asked more questions, but I didn't. You know how us men are when it comes to a woman. Now I have to share this with you, and, as always, I have to be honest. Because of my accident, my memory is a little off, but it's still there. I am 100 percent sure that this happen. I just don't remember the exact time. I think it was before the car theft, but I'm not completely sure. Either way, I will share.

I was at work, and there was this girl I really liked, so I asked her out on a date. The plan was to take her out in my friend's car. The date went extremely well, and we ended up at a park, making out. While we were at the park, a police officer rolled up in his patrol car. He asked for my identification. I provided it, and everything was fine. He ran the license plate on the car I was in, and all of a sudden I was thrown onto the hood of the car and handcuffed. Apparently, the car I'd borrowed had been used in a recent home invasion. I was not aware of anything related to this, and I sure wasn't part of it. I might have been a criminal at this time, but I never did anything to harm or hurt anyone.

Obviously, both the girl and I were arrested. Definitely not the date she had in mind. We were both in an interrogation room, for hours. What was I going to do? I told them the truth—that

I'd borrowed the car and was not aware of anything to do with a stolen car, much less a home invasion.

This was the second time I was arrested for an auto theft, and again I was being let go. They were forced to let me go because, apparently, they were looking for an Asian man who'd committed the crime. They knew I was not part of it. I again was set free, but this time, I was not taken home. I found my own way home.

How many people do you know that have been arrested twice for such a crime and let go. As this story continues, you will read that there might be a purpose to all of this.

After this mess and a few others, I decided I was not the kind of man I wanted to be, and that was not the kind if life I wanted to have. So I went to work and went back to my roots— dancing salsa. Since we're Puerto Rican, dancing and music have always been very big in my family. This is true of most families in Puerto Rico. We are not a Spanish country, yet our music is heard worldwide. I have to say, we have

artists like El Grand Combo and Marc Anthony
in salsa, Don Omar and Farruko in reggaeton.
My father was a very good salsa dancer. My
mother, my aunts, even both my grandmas are
all very good dancers, but my father was specifically known for being a good dancer. He also
was a conga player, but that's another story. My
mom's younger sister, Millie, had a boyfriend
named Fred. He was a professional salsa dancer
and instructor at the time and a good friend.
Fred, wherever you are, hello, friend! I started
taking classes and learning from him. It wasn't
long before I was his assistant and helping him
teach his class at a local club. Mind you, the club
was for people twenty-one and over. I was only
seventeen at this time and not old enough to be
there, but since Fred worked there, they didn't
ask me any questions when I walked in.

Fred's dance partner and instructor, a girl
named Adriana, became my partner—in more
than just dancing. She was teaching her daugh-
ters and me a dance routine. I would dance in
the middle of the girl group. Also as part of our

routine, the girls would take turns dancing with me, the only guy. We entered a contest at a local festival. We were set to walk and dance as we moved along through the downtown streets. I'm happy to say we won that contest. It was a new experience for me and a new accomplishment. Dancing salsa became my thing. It still is.

Up until my accident, I'd always gone dancing. My wife and I tried to go out dancing as often as we could. After my accident, it is actually what I missed doing the most. I'm thirty-eight now, and I still love salsa dancing. I would say it's my passion.

After that contest, my aunt Millie and I started prepping for the next contest. This is where the moment of fame on international TV comes in. Latin MTV on Telemundo was going from city to city at the time and holding salsa contests at the local clubs. I practiced lots with my aunt and Fred. We were practicing flares, shines, and dips. I crack up because I remember dropping my aunt Millie during one of those dip practices. Poor thing, I dropped her on the back of her neck once. Not my best moment, but funny as heck. Sorry, Aunty! She was not seriously hurt, thank God, just sore from the drop. We cracked up but continued. We practiced and practiced and practiced. The night of the show I was so excited I parked the car but left my CD case on the passenger seat. When we got out, I noticed my CD case had been stolen. What the heck? I didn't care though. I'd just danced on international TV with my aunt.

Unfortunately, this was not like the festival. We did not win first place on this one, but we had a lot of fun preparing and dancing for the actual event. Heck, even getting my huge CD case stolen at the time was fun. We laughed and laughed—all part of the story.

Remember Adriana the dance instructor? Remember her becoming my partner in more than just dancing? Well as you can imagined, Adriana and I spent a lot of time prepping and dancing for the contests. We started liking each other. I mean, let's be real. She was a very attractive woman and a dancer. What man wouldn't like that? So I already liked her. What I should say is that, thankfully, she started liking me back. There was a problem there though. She was a lot older than me. I was seventeen at the time; she was thirty-two years old. Big difference. None of us intended for that to happen, especially not her, of course. But we started seeing each other. She made it very clear that it could never be serious, because of the age difference. No problem, at the time. I understood that. She was just someone I was just hanging out with.

During this time, I went through one big important moment in my life. Fred and I were teaching a class on Sunday night where we frequently taught every Sunday. As the class ended I saw this beautiful, dark-skinned woman walking away from the class. I asked her to dance. Twenty-one years later, we're still dancing. That beautiful, dark-skinned woman ended up being my wife. I was in a twenty-one-and-over club. My wife will be upset for me sharing this with you, but naturally she is older than me—four years older to be exact. I was seventeen, and she was twenty-one. Now that I think about it, I guess being with an older woman was kind of my thing. First it was my older sister's best friend, Blondie. Then it was Adriana the dance instructor. Then my wife, Darling, the dark-skinned girl at the club. I liked the older girls, I guess.

Adriana and I had been going out for about a year or so. I went against our oral agreement of not taking it seriously because of the age difference. I told Adriana that I really liked her and that I didn't care about the age difference. She reminded me that we were just hanging out. She told me she did care about our age difference and that we could not take it serious. Therefore, there was not a serious agreement.

When I saw Darling walking away from the dance class, I prowled on her like an animal hunting its prey. Adriana saw Darling and I talking and got really upset. Later that same night, I drove over to Adriana house, and she was obviously still upset. I was a little surprised because of how she'd reacted when I told her I really liked her. Anyway, Adriana and I talked, and we basically put things to an end. We would never see each other intimately again. On the other hand, Darling and I really hit it off. We started dating at this point, and twenty-one years later, we're still at it.

Dancing and teaching salsa has followed me all the way through my life. Even in Florida. I decided to move. I wanted a fresh start and to leave my bad past behind me. My choices were Seattle or Florida. I didn't have anybody in Seattle, but it was a city I always wanted to visit and, possibly, to live in. I chose Florida because my father's family—grandparents, aunts, and cousins—were living there by then. When you're moving to a new place, it's always good to be somewhat familiar, even if it's with people. Actually, it's especially important to know people. Funny thing is I actually made it to Seattle later for all the right reasons, but again, we will get to that shortly.

At the time, I really had no reason to move. I had a great job, making really good money. I worked for a semiconductor company as a document control manager. I wrote procedures for over fifteen departments. I was around twenty at the time. I didn't have any big responsibilities. I made really good money, but I wanted a fresh start, and as with other things in my life, I made it happen.

It's a long drive from California to Florida, but I decided to drive. What a lot of fun that was. I drove across country with my brother-in-law. I guess my deciding to move motivated my older sister to want to come along. She actually moved first. Her husband and I decided drive next. He and I drove to Florida in two separate cars. We each took a walkie-talkie, and they were our means of communication with each other the entire trip. It took a total of five days. Ordinarily, we could have done it in about two days, even stopping to rest, but we spent some time in places along the way.

I strongly suggest everybody drive across country at least once in their lifetime. It shows you how beautiful this country we call home really is. There were some must-do things I really had to do while driving across country. They were things I'd previously said I was going do if I ever drove across country. Number one was going to the Grand Canyon. This was a must-see for me, and, man, was it worth it. The Grand Canyon was everything I'd imagined it to be and more. It was absolutely beautiful. A breathtaking experience. I just can't comment on that enough. Beautiful!

The second thing was (and remember, I was and Elvis fan—still am) going to Elvis's house in Memphis, Tennessee. An absolute must-do. On the way to Tennessee, around Oklahoma, my brother-in-law's Camaro had some engine problems, but thankfully we were able to fix them. A few hundred dollars in repairs later, we moved on. That's why it took three days longer. One day in the Grand Canyon, one day with car problems, and one day in Memphis.

We arrived in Memphis at night, but I couldn't wait. I had to see it. Before going to the hotel where we would spend the night, we went to Graceland, Elvis's house. For years, I'd dreamed of visiting the place. I couldn't believe I was there. We got there around ten at night, and it was obviously closed, but I was able to see it, and we chatted with the security guard at the fence for a while. I got to ask some questions and get some internal information from the guard. Some very good things to hear.

What can I tell you about Graceland? Super cool. It was really cool to see the luxuries of a rich person back in that day. Also, as you can imagine, Elvis was not your normal rich person. He definitely had his own style. Across the street from Graceland is a museum housing what used to be his private car collection. I mean, it was a beautiful collection of cars. The man definitely had taste. We spent all day there. I could have spent a lot more than just that day, but I had to behave. My brother-in-law was with me. We continued our trip and arrived in Florida the next night.

FLORIDA

Florida was definitely a change from California. Everything was different—the lifestyle, cost of living, people. To be honest, when I first got to Florida, I hated it. I hated everything about it. When I arrived, my grandparents allowed me to move in with them—my father's parents that I used to live in the same neighborhood with in Puerto Rico. My grandmother, my father's mom, has always been, and thankfully still is, one of the biggest loves of my life. I didn't waste any time. I stayed with them for about two months.

I worked on getting settled and on a job right away, before bringing Darling over. My older sister, Yaritza, moved over a short time before, so we got a place together. My little sister stayed with Mom in California. We rented a huge house. I had a job by then, so things were moving forward. Yaritza and Joe didn't waste any time. They got jobs right away as well. In California, to rent a house like the one we rented would have cost a fortune. The house had four bedrooms and three baths. Big and beautiful. Yaritza and I eventually went our separate ways and got our own places with our families and continued working.

I had a few jobs over the years. My last eight to five job was working as a human resource manager for a demolition company. I did payroll, human resources, and permitting. I used to pull the permits for new demolition projects at the city or county office, depending on project location. When that employment came to an end, I decided to start my first company, providing permitting service for other construction companies, including the demolition company I used to work for. My company was called X-celerated Permits. I was working on getting the company off ground and having steady income. Unfortunately, at that time I wasn't bringing in enough income to cover living expenses, so I decided to go back to work. I applied for a temporary agency and they got me an assignment at a local drug and DNA testing facility. The testing facility was not doing too well at the time. The owner had me there to perform a lot of the cleanup, and he really seemed to be prepping for the company to shut down, since no new business was coming in. He seemed to be struggling to hold on to the little business he had.

In order to help him and the business, I recommended the demolition company that was my former employer and my permit client at the time. I called the owner of the demo company, and because I knew they did drug testing prior to hiring anybody, I told the owner I was now working for a drug testing company and could help him when he needed those services, and he agreed.

He started using our service, but as time went on, the demo company called me to complain. They were not being serviced on time. Our drug testers were not even showing up for appointments. The customer was not happy. I referred this company from the bottom of my heart in order to help the company I was working for. I wanted to help them have a future. Well, as time went on, I noticed that, more and more, the drug testing company I was working for was not fulfilling their part of the deal. I had a really good relationship with the owner and the demo company I used to work for. I do still. It's not easy to turn your former employer into a client. There was a lot of confidence in me, and I was not going to allow that relationship to be ruined. Therefore, I decided to take over. I started my own drug and DNA testing company, with the demo company as my own first client. My good intentions paid off. I turned my company into a business with over a million dollars yearly revenue. Then I moved on.

I called it X-celerated DNA and Drug Screenings. I even ran commercials and ads. Very cool things. I even put my daughter's picture on one of the ads. I now owned two companies, and there was no need to work for anyone anymore. I found an officemate and moved into our own office. My officemate had a temporary work agency like the one that got me the assignment with the drug testing company. The businesses were both doing well. The new office even better. Things were moving forward in an orderly fashion.

Darling and I were not married yet, but we had been together for about seven years. Not that there was anything bad going on. We were just busy living, and honestly we didn't think about it. Darling comes from a very Catholic family, so I knew it was important to her to be married, but as time went on, it just turned out to be something we didn't talk or even think about. We sat and talked one day and we decided to have a child. My son Isaiah was born soon after. As you can imagine, having a baby boy brought lots of joy. Being a new father was and is still an amazing feeling. My son was obviously planned.

Fortunately, three years later, Darling, Isaiah, and I went to California on vacation to visit her mom. One of the days we were out there was Darling's birthday. Isaiah stayed with my mother-in-law. Naturally, Darling and I went out to celebrate. Many margaritas later, our gorgeous daughter was conceived. We had not taken precautions, and soon after, Zeani was born. We were now a full family. Darling and I were leaving with two beautiful children. Zeani was conceived in California but born in Florida. Zeani, you were the best accident in my life.

Back to business. Funny how things work out. My office roommate found herself in the same situation as the drug testing company. Her company was not doing too well. At the time, she was dead in the water, meaning she had no business, no prospects, just not doing well at all. So here I came again, honestly, with the best intentions in the world. She was my office roommate at the time. Naturally I want to help her get business and pay her rent so that we can continue our relationship and move forward. I again called the demo company, my permit and drug testing client, and I said I had access to laborers and that we were available as a labor company if needed. As I worked for them as an

HR manager, I was fully aware that they often used laborers. We made an offer and, thankfully, they accepted. We were now their new labor company, and I was now running three companies. Permit, drug testing, and labor. I went from working full time to running and supervising three companies in a very short period of time. Many thanks to Pece of Mind Demolition (Pece being the last name of the owner of the company). They are an awesome demolition company. Out of all the construction companies I have worked for and with, they are by far the most organized and capable of handling your project accurately, on time, and safely. Thank you for all the peace of mind.

A few years passed. My son was now around seven or eight years old, and my daughter was around four or five. I went through the worst experience in my life. To this day I still have a hard time just writing or talking about it. My mother got sick. She was diagnosed with breast cancer. She lived in Las Vegas at the time. By then, my older sister had moved to Vegas. So both of my sisters and my mother lived in Las Vegas at the time. My older sister, Yaritza, younger sister, Denisse, and my mother, Clara, followed the organic lifestyle and eating habits. I could say I was living a somewhat organic lifestyle too. For example, the meat and eggs I ate had to be organic, but not everything, as it was with my mother and sisters. I was not as strict with it as they were. Anyway, my mother was diagnosed, and she and my sisters decided to check her into a cancer clinic located in Tijuana, Mexico, were they followed the natural way of medicine more than in the United States. My sisters didn't want Mom to have chemotherapy or anything close to that. My mother felt the same way. I, of course, supported my mother and sisters and didn't argue. I wasn't educated in the options enough at the time to make a smarter decision. And again, I would have supported their decision either way. So they decided to check her into that cancer clinic. Out of the three of us siblings, I was the only one that had a fairly flexible schedule. I owned my own businesses, while my sisters had full-time jobs. So I could get away a lot easier. We decided I would go with mom to Mexico. I left my businesses under the care of my office partner/officemate, Darling. She was awesome enough to stay with our kids while I went to take care of Mom. So I flew to Las Vegas, we rented a vehicle, and I drove down to the clinic in Mexico with Mom to check her in.

Mexico was an experience. We were at a private clinic. Everyone was very nice and helpful. Much love and respect to the Rubio Cancer Clinic in Mexico. Thank you! I was there for a total of three and a half months. I came home to visit my woman and kids once during that time for a week, but then I went back with Mom.

One day, I asked for permission to take Mom out. I wanted to spend a day just her and I. The driver took us to the beach. We had lunch there and walked around. We had a great time. I somehow knew to take advantage of time with Mom. It would turn out be the last day I would spend with her. She got fatigued from walking, so I had to carry her to the car and up a hill at the beach. Back at the clinic, Mom got very ill after this. She fell into a coma. I called my sisters and told them the situation and urged them to hurry down. Thankfully, when they got there, she was still alive. In a coma, but alive. They got to see her and say their goodbyes, as I did. Unfortunately, she never regained consciousness from that coma. She passed away. My mother was a very special woman and mom. It's been six years since we lost her, and I still feel it like it was yesterday. I got to see her one more time recently, but we will talk about that shortly.

To all you children out there, love your mom, appreciate your mom, and be good to her. Tell her you love her. Let her now you care for her. Losing my mother has been one of the worst experiences in my life. These were very difficult times for me.

Unfortunately, life had to continue without her. We decided to cremate her. We left Mexico with my mom in a damn box. We took the bus back to Las Vegas from the Tijuana border, and what a ride that was. Eventually I went back to Florida and moved forward. I went back to work.

As I'm writing my story about my mother and the horrible disease, I got a call from one of my good friend's sons, telling me that his father, who I knew had cancer, was in his last days. My friend asked that I go see him. His father, Ruben, used to be my neighbor next to the first house I ever bought in my life. He's a little bit older than me. He's seventy-nine years old now, and I'm thirty-eight, but that doesn't matter. He has always been a good friend. I just went to pay him a visit with my family. I'm sorry, but I cried like a little girl on the way home. It was completely devastating to see him in that condition. That horrible disease is getting the best of us. It got the best of my mother and is getting the best of my good friend, Ruben, and many more. We have to be more careful with the food and water we put into our bodies, as well as with the medicines we use. They add so much crap and chemicals to all these things that I believe that's a major contributor to the success of this horrible disease. As this story continues, you will have a true example of how important it is to try a minimized these things away in your body. You'll see how important it really is to your health to keep that non-organic crap out of your body. It's definitely made a difference in my recuperation and my life. Later, in my organic living chapter, you'll have more of an opportunity to read about this hugely important issue that we seem to be ignoring. Organic food and living is definitely a better alternative to what we have going on nowadays. My prayers and best wishes go out to Ruben and his family.

A couple of days after I received the news of my friend Ruben. I got a call from the owner of one of my three largest company clients for X-celerated Solutions. He told me his oldest son had just been in a motorcycle accident similar to mine and was in a coma. (At the time of the writing of this book, he was still in a coma.) I'm already using my experience for something positive. I put my wife on the phone, and because of what she had been through with me, she was able to recommend the hospital I was in, Brooks Rehabilitation Hospital, in Jacksonville, Florida. She also gave him organic food recommendations, and she suggested rose pedals be kept in his room so that he could smell them while in coma, as they did for me. Interestingly, the scent of rose pedals stimulates your brain while in coma, so it's good to have that scent nearby. My wife also recommended the reflexologist that used to massage my feet while I was in coma. My sisters and Darling did everything possible for my well-being. Apparently, your feet mimic your brain. Therefore getting a foot massage is similar to getting a brain massage. I have to be honest. I even had this done after I woke up. I can't tell you how great it felt. It was so mind relaxing and comfortable. I feel good knowing that our new knowledge and experience allows us to provide useful information to others in a similar situation and in need. It feels great to be able to help.

Remember my officemate? She did a great job keeping the business going. I can't complain.

She was great, but unfortunately, she started failing on labor orders from our clients. I started to receive complaints, especially from the demo company again, and I was forced to make a change. I kept the labor service. This was never my intention. It really just worked out this way. I now owned three companies. Two of them were started with the best intentions. I had X-celerated Permits, X-celerated DNA and Drug Screenings, and the labor company, which I called X-celerated Solutions. I kept working and focusing on growing my businesses. Believe it or not, I grew the heck out of X-celerated Solutions. In less than a year, I was the labor company for four of the largest demo companies in Central Florida. I grew my labor company to over 160 employees—seven in the office and 157 in the field. Out of the 157 employees, I had thirty of them remodeling hotels across country. I had two groups of fifteen, each traveling across country and remodeling hotels. The other 127 employees were laborers only. Basically I worked like a staffing agency. I would send you employees to help you as the client with the work at hand, and I billed by the hour. But unlike a temp agency, my employees were mine full time. They were not trying to get a job with my client, they were just there to help the client with the work. I got two hotels to remodel in Seattle. Naturally, as the owner starting and growing a company, I wanted to see the project first hand. So I had to travel to Seattle. A few weeks later, since I was so fond of Seattle, I brought Darling over. I took her shopping for a dress, and we went salsa dancing and had a great time. What a great city. Darling and I loved it.

Back to work again. My DNA and drug testing company had its own office. I had my younger sister, Denisse, running that company with three other employees. Denisse, in so many ways, would become one of my heroes. X-celerated Permits was my first and smallest company. Because of the type of service it was, I was the only one that would do that. I had my office employees help me from time to time, but mostly it was only me. Last but not least, I had X-celerated Solutions, my labor company. It was the largest company out of all three. So I had two offices with three companies. I had my DNA and drug screening company, with four employees and it's on own office, run by Denisse. I had Solutions, with 164 employees and its own office, as well with seven employees working in that office. It was a big office with a reception area, four separate office suites, its own kitchen, a large room used for training, and a shop for tools. I also had the permitting company, which shared the office with Solutions. The two companies also shared one employee—me.

I had my companies running strong for a little over ten years. In 2015, what used to be my three little businesses sold over six million dollars. Not bad for a former high school dropout and trouble maker. By the way, when I got to be an independent adult, one of the first things I made sure to do was obtain my GED. If I wanted to do something with my life, that was a must. That's the way I did it, but in no way, shape, or form would I suggest anyone do what I did. School is a must. It's a tool you will use to become a better person, a more business oriented person, a self-obtained person. Do not take school lightly. Everything I used to create, grow, and run my companies was learned in one place. School! Yes, I was a high school dropout, but it was my focus and determination and education that brought me to where I eventually arrived. I had built my own enterprise. X-celerated Enterprises.

I moved my family into a five-bedroom, four-bath home on a lake. I bought three motorcycles—a Harley, a Hayabusa, and a dirt bike. I bought my children dirt bikes as well. My kids, Zeani and Isaiah, were both riders before they were ten years old. Next to the lake our house was on, there was a lot of available land for them to ride. They absolutely loved taking their bikes out and riding. Not for nothing, but my daughter is a heck of a rider. She's born to ride. My son likes it as well, but with my daughter, you can tell it's more than just riding. It's her passion. I wonder where she gets that from? I also went and bought a brand new ninety thousand dollar BMW and a new Toyota Tundra. Now, material things don't matter. I share this with you in order to give you a better idea of how far I had gotten in life and where I was standing at the time. Again, family was doing great, business was also doing great, finances even better. I can tell you that I was able to go out and spend two thousand in a week's time like nothing, not have to worry about it. Life was comfortable at the time.

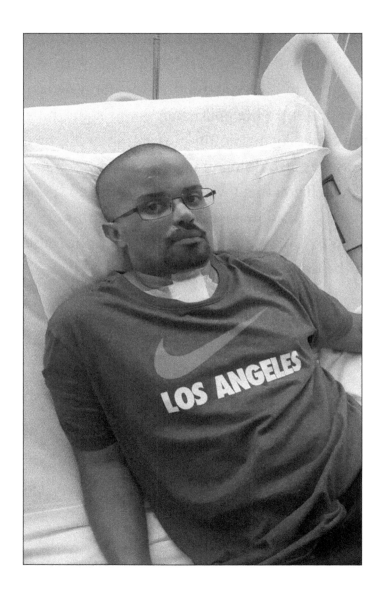

MY TESTIMONY

I woke up in an enclosed bed in the hospital with both of my sisters and Darling looking right at me. I woke up in a strange bed, strange place. I felt very odd.

"What happen?" I said. "What's going on?"

Imagine this for a second. Out of nowhere, you just wake up not knowing where the heck you are. You're in a strange place and a strange bed. Apparently, months have gone by without you knowing about it.

I had to learn to breath on my own again. I had to learn to walk again. Everything. Just like a newborn baby. I was new to life all over again. I was reborn.

I had no recollection of how I got into that situation. To be honest, I still don't. I don't have any memory of what really happened. I can only go by what I've been told. My sisters and

Darling explained to me that I was in a bad accident and that I'd just awakened from a two-month coma. My mind was confused; my whole body was confused. I really didn't know what was going on. They told me that Darling and I were in a bad motorcycle accident. A girl talking on her phone had pulled out in front of me and made me crash into her. Apparently, I was in Jacksonville, Florida, miles from home, in a hospital that specialized in my injury—head trauma. I was just finding all this out for the first time. Apparently, Darling, Jose, and I left the house on a Saturday night to go out for the night, and unfortunately we never came home. Jose was one of my best employees and friends at the time. He used to be Denisse's boyfriend, but when their relationship came to an end, I let him live with us and continue working with me. Not what I would normally do with one of my sisters exes, but he was a good man, a good employee, and a good friend. Plus Jose and Denisse's relationship was none of my business. As long as he didn't hurt or put his hands on my sister, we were okay. Anyway, we went out that night to go pick up his date. Darling and I were riding my V-rod Harley, and Jose was riding my best friend's Suzuki Boulevard, which he kept in my garage. We were on the way to pick up his date, and this girl in a Mitsubishi Montero was pulling out of her neighborhood. She basically pulled right in front of me.

My friend Jose told me that before I crashed, he saw me elbow Darling, knocking her off the bike. He was in shock when I elbowed her because he didn't know I was about to crash. I elbowed Darling off the bike, cracking the top left part of her head open. She also broke two ribs, her wrist, and her clavicle bone. Only God knows, but I possibly saved her life. After this mess, she got out of the hospital in one day. If you ask me, she was lucky. She was not the same case as me.

Unfortunately, I crashed and went flat line. I died and, thankfully, was brought back. Reborn! I got a copy of the ambulance report. It states that when I was picked up, I was not breathing.

I was given CPR in the ambulance and revived on the way to the hospital. Jose also told me I was lying dead on the ground before the ambulance came, and the girl that pulled out in front of me was still on the phone. A cop who arrived on the scene saw her. "Get off the phone," he yelled. Can you believe that? They kill you but stay on the phone.

I fell into a coma. While I was in the coma, the doctors told Darling and my two sisters that I had 90 percent impairment and that if and when I woke up, I would be a vegetable. It was not even certain that I'd even wake up from coma. Those were the chances they were giving me. This is one of those times that you can actually be glad the doctors were wrong. I woke up from a two-month coma. Two months! By the way, while in coma, I had to be fed, I had to be changed—just like a newborn baby.

I am sorry. I have to touch base on this once again. I was a grown, thirty-six-year-old man at the time. I woke up in a strange place, apparently months later. Strange bed, strange everything.

No memory whatsoever of how I got there. I had a breathing tube in my throat and a feeding tube in my stomach. I didn't know how to stand, how to walk. I was wearing a diaper. I realized I was in a hospital.

I looked at my sisters. "What the heck is going on? Where am I?" I said.

Unless you've been through this, you can't imagine what waking up from a coma is like. I don't care who you are. This would be weird for anybody, but that's how I woke up.

Darling went and got our beautiful children. I got to see my family again. After I woke up, I was at the hospital two or three days, and they let me go home. I was able to walk out of my room, shake hands with the doctors, and thank the staff and nurses.

I always think about one particular lady. I'm sorry I didn't get her name, but she was a nurse there. She was one of the many nurses that used to attend to me. I remember this so well that I can draw you a picture of her, her surroundings, everything. She came up to me very serious, pointed a finger at me, and said, "You better say a prayer of thanks that you're getting out of here walking the way you are. Do you know how many people we see here that unfortunately are not as blessed as you are?"

Now, remember, I was in a hospital that specialized in injuries like mine. Head trauma. Almost everybody on the floor I was on was in a coma. Much love and respect to Brooks Rehabilitation Hospital, in Jacksonville, FL. Thank you for your hard work and dedication. I would not be here if it wasn't for your doctors, nurses, and staff. Thank you so very much! On another note, I can't help but think sometimes that I was given a second chance in life because I sacrificed myself to save Darling. What do you think?

Well, I got to go home. As you can imagine the accident impacted our finances quite a bit. My BMW was in the garage. My sisters had sold all my motorcycles except the wrecked Harley. Everything else at home was normal for the moment. Darling knew I just wasn't able to go back to work right away, and since our finances were not the same, she was forced to make arrangements to move to a smaller, more affordable house. Thankfully she was able to keep us in the same neighborhood. We loved our area and our kids' school. Moving meant all of that changing. Darling was awesome enough to find us a house down the street. It was a three-bedroom, two-bath home.

We got some moving help. Prior to this, we went to give my BMW back. We kept the Tundra as our main vehicle. It had a full-size crew cab, so we could all fit comfortably there, including our gorgeous dog—a beautiful English sheep dog I consider my third child.

The BMW was just a car, but getting it had been a huge accomplishment for me. As part of my clean-up project prior to starting my businesses, I'd filed for bankruptcy. Then I diligently and with great focused worked on rebuilding my credit. In less than a year's time from bankruptcy, I was in a BMW dealership buying a ninety-thousand-dollar BMW. I was the first person in my family ever to own a luxury car or a car of that quality. I was very sad to sell it, but it had to be done. Well, we moved, got settled in the new home, and we focused on my beautiful children. I tried and am still trying very hard to live a somewhat normal life and get everything back in order. I'm far from making that last part happen at this specific time, but I'm alive.

Also, one more thing I have to touch base on. Remember my grandfather, the one that let me stay with him when I came to Florida? Him and my grandmother that I lived in the same neighborhood with in Puerto Rico. I always absolutely loved all my grandparents, but this particular grandfather and I became very close over the years I lived in Florida. I've lived in Florida since 2000. Visiting my grandparents, even when I moved out, was a must-do for me. Darling used to help Grandma cooked for a religious marriage retreat. My father's family was and still is very involved with church. So we also used to go over to their house about once a month and stay over the weekend while the ladies cooked. I loved spending time with my grandparents.

My grandfather was handicapped from birth. He could walk but not for long. He was born with his feet completely backward, and in his day, all they could do was brake them, set them straight, and let them heal that way. He walked with a limp. As he got older, walking got harder for him, so he needed a hoover lift and a medical bed at home. Nothing against his children, but out of seven kids, thirteen grandkids, the only people that had the ability at work and took the time for Grandpa were my Aunt Digna and I. Aunt Digna helps them tremendously. I took the time out of my busy life then to go purchase his hoover, his medical bed, and whatever else he needed. Anything for Grandpa. I was extremely close to him, and he was very important.

I don't know if this was a dream or what, but while I was in a coma, my grandfather came to see me. He was walking down the street approaching an intersection with a four-way stop. I stared at him because I was surprised he was walking normally. He was wearing black pants, black boots, and a black guayabera (a traditional Puerto Rican shirt). In life he was a very firm man with a very strong character. This was not the type of man you would want to mess with. In the dream, he came right up to me and put his finger in front of my face. He told me in Spanish, "Get the heck up, stop playing around, and pay attention to this woman."

Remember my sisters, and my grandma— the woman in my life? At this point, this is when I woke up from my two-month coma. I think about this every day. When I woke up from my coma, the first thing I told Darling was that I wanted to see Grandpa.

She gave me a very serious look. "You don't remember?" she said. "He passed away before your accident."

I had to think it over. Finally, I remembered. He passed away six months before my accident, but I did not remember until Darling reminded me. It was like I lost him all over again.

I saw my mom under the same condition, I guess, in a dream or whatever it was. But in the dream, I knew she'd passed away. I know today that she talked to me, but I somehow also know that I'm not supposed to remember what she talked to me about.

I did see both her and Grandpa clear as day. They both tried to wake me up from my coma. I think about this every day. For some reason, I also know my grandfather got in trouble for waking me up or for what he did to wake me up. Funny thing is, my grandfather was a by-the-book man. He always followed the rules. But for some reason, I think he broke one or some to help me wake up. Thinking about this boggles my mind all the time. I think about this every day. I love and miss them both immensely.

Now, I died August 6, 2016. My accident was after eleven at night, but the ambulance didn't get there until after midnight, so it was on the seventh. Therefore, I was not revived until August 7, 2016, which is my official accident date. I've been told I wasn't breathing for about fifteen minutes or so. Unbelievable. I had head trauma, and the minimum time for recovery from a head trauma is five years. It's been three years, and I'm still recuperating, but I'm fighting hard to get back, close to or even better than I was. God willing! This experience hasn't been easy for any of us. Not for Darling, for my sisters, and especially not for me.

LIVING ORGANIC

While I was in a coma, my sisters and Darling did not agree with the food and water the hospital was giving me, which was mostly canned food, and water from the sink. Being the awesome women the three of them are, they wanted to provide me with organic food and water. Of course, I had a feeding tube in my stomach, through which the food was administered. The hospital would not allow them to do alter my diet without signing a waiver. Basically they had to sign a form stating that if they fed me organic items, the hospital was not responsible, which I understand. I have nothing against the hospital or their methods. My wife and sisters just felt I would benefit more at that time from the organic foods, and they were right.

They went out and purchased organic food, organic water, and a water dispenser. For the next two months, they fed me organic food and water. Remember, the doctors had said there was a 90 percent chance that I would be a vegetable when I woke up, if I ever did. Well, only God knows why, but I was able to get up and walk out of my room when I woke up, and there was only a 10 percent chance I'd be able to do that. The doctors and nurses saw cases like mine on a daily basis. They called me Miracle Patient. I can't tell you that the organic food was the reason, but I can tell you that the methods of my wife and sisters definitely contributed to my well-being, had a positive impact on my recovery, and made a major difference in my results.

Eating organic definitely makes a difference. It allows us to get the benefits from the food we eat as intended. It impacts your health, your energy levels, and obviously your recovery, as it did for me. Because this happened to me, I couldn't help but Google "organic food success stories." The results were surprising. Google the same phrase, and it will have you fully convinced that organic foods definitely make a difference. Think about this for a second. Even beer companies are advertising and selling organic beer. Why? They know this is a growing issue and more and more people are realizing that the issue with non-organic food needs to be addressed. I believe more and more people are starting to realize that this is a hugely ignored problem. But there aren't yet enough people learning about it. I'd been eating semi-organic food before the accident. I made sure my meats and eggs were organic. I didn't care as much for all other items. I didn't really have a reason to do that, but that was my preference, even before knowing what I know now. I've addressed it. I am addressing it now.

I'm educating my children in organic eating habits. When you plant a plant in the wrong kind of dirt, it may grow, but not as fast or as strong. How does the right kind of food impact your child when growing? They put so many chemicals in foods nowadays. Whether it's for more volume or what, I don't know, but it's definitely not meant for our bodies.

I want to share with you the benefits and why I think it's completely worth it to go organic. There is a difference in cost. It's slightly more expensive to go with the organic option, but it's completely worth it. Come on, people, when it comes to your health, is money really that important? Money or health? How your life will be impacted will make a big difference. The taste, the way you feel, the impact it has in your life, it's amazing.

Here are some much needed facts: Organic produce contains fewer pesticides. Organic food is often fresher. Organic farming is better for the environment. Organically raised animals are *not* given antibiotics, growth hormones, or fed animal byproducts. Organic meat and milk are richer in certain nutrients. Organic food is GMO-free.

"How your food is grown or raised can have a major impact on your mental and emotional health as well as the environment. Organic foods often have more beneficial nutrients, such as antioxidants, than their conventionally-grown counterparts, and people with allergies to foods, chemicals, or preservatives often find their symptoms lessen or go away when they eat only organic foods.

"The ongoing debate about the effects of GMOs on health and the environment is a controversial one. In most cases, GMOs are engineered to make food crops resistant to herbicides and/or to produce an insecticide. For example, much of the sweet corn consumed in the US is genetically engineered to be resistant to the herbicide Roundup and to produce its own insecticide, Bt Toxin.

"GMOs are also commonly found in US crops such as soybeans, alfalfa, squash, zucchini, papaya, and canola, and are present in many breakfast cereals and much of the processed food that we eat. If the ingredients on a package include corn syrup or soy lecithin, chances are it contains GMOs.

"GMOs and pesticides The use of toxic herbicides like Roundup (glyphosate) has increased fifteen times since GMOs were introduced. While the World Health Organization announced that glyphosate is 'probably carcinogenic to humans,' there is still some controversy over the level of health risks posed by the use of pesticides."

Please educate yourself in these facts and many more. Living organic definitely makes a difference in you, your body, your health. Something to look into.

AFTERMATH

Wow, the aftermath. Where do I start. One of the side effects I've had to deal with has to do with my short-term memory. Don't worry; everything I've told you is true, but I have no recollection whatsoever of the accident or anything close to that date. I also tend to forget recent things often. Sometimes I remind myself, sometimes other things do. You should see the reminders on my phone. I even downloaded an additional phone app that I use to make notes and remember things.

So we moved to the new home. We were trying to get settled. Jose was still living with us but moved out shortly after. We had a maid living with us in the bigger house, and we had to let her go as well. One of the first things I needed to do to feel somewhat back to normal was, for some reason, drive. I was feeling good and capable. I had a good friend of mine ride with me around the neighborhood in one of my company trucks to see how I did. I played around with him. I had him wear a motorcycle helmet, even while we were riding inside the truck, "just in case."

I mentioned earlier that Denisse was one of my heroes. Actually, Denisse, Yaritza, and Darling all were heroes to me. When I was in a coma, I was not legally married, so my significant other, Darling, didn't have full authority to make decisions regarding my condition. My sisters did. While I was on life support, the doctors asked my sisters if they wanted to disconnect me and, basically, just let me die. My sisters said, "Heck no. We'll take him however we can get him."

Also, at the time of my accident, while I was in a coma, Denisse and Yaritza sold everything in the Solutions office. My company had fallen into debt shortly before my accident, or so I've been told. I have no recollection of this. Apparently, one of my biggest clients for the hotel renovations fell into debt with me. They fell behind by about eighty-five thousand dollars. That's a lot of money. Naturally, I fell behind as well. For some reason, I got hit all at once. I also had another client that owed me around thirty thousand and another that owed me around three thousand. That was a little over a hundred K all at once.

For the first time, I fell behind on payroll. My guys remodeling the hotels had a lot of faith and trust in me, so they kept working while I repaired my problems. Unfortunately, due to my accident, I never fully got the opportunity. Anyway, by the time my accident happened, I was seventy-two thousand behind on payroll. So after the accident, Denisse and Yaritza sold company property and equipment and worked to pay down that debt. When I woke up, about 95 percent of the debt had been paid.

Denisse and Yaritza joked around with me, but they looked at me very seriously when they said, "You've had the life for a while, and when things finally go bad for you, you sleep through the entire problem." In a way they're right. My businesses where running strong, and when they didn't get into problems until my accident happened. Having the awesome strong, smart independent women that I get to call sisters, this problem came to an end while in coma. My sisters were and are incredible enough to deal with my condition while at the same time taking care of business and everything else. By the way, during this time, I called the company that owed me eighty-five K or so, and they paid me after some very serious threats over the telephone. Also, the company that owed me about three grand, we took them to court and won. I happen to have a younger cousin who's an attorney, and he is a bad ass. We won that case, and they were forced to pay. Up to this point I have gotten back payments from two out of three companies that owed me and made my world and life impossible. My cousin Felix and I are working on the third one as we speak. Wish us luck. Many thanks to Felix Montanez Law Firm, in Tampa, Florida. If you need a good attorney in the Tampa area, look him up. He's definitely worth it.

Well, here is where we might agree on the reason for my accident, or we might not. My companies fell into debt for the first time in over ten years. As a person and businessman, I've have always helped tons of people. Many times, I've given jobs and opportunities to those that were down. I took time to train people with no experience, get them going, and put them to work. Many of these guys had families, including children to support, and I made sure they were able to do that.

So what was happening to my companies and why? I felt I didn't deserve what was happening. I would pray and pray and ask God, "Why, why is this happening to me? Get me out of this mess, Lord. Help me get people's lives back in order."

Since my accident, people like to tell me how sorry they are that this happen to me. Or they make comments and ask, "Why, Lord? Why this guy?"

I'm speaking from the bottom of my heart when I say that I don't think what happen to me was completely an accident. I believe the accident was an answer to my prayers. I believe it was God's way to get me out of the mess with my businesses. These are not new feelings. I've felt like this ever since the accident.

The accident was horrible. The recuperation has been just as bad and longer. I read somewhere that it normally takes head trauma patients five years to recover. It was three years for me seven days ago. My entire life changed in fifteen minutes—my professional life and my personal life. It has affected my children, my wife, my siblings, but my faith in God does not fade.

I strongly believe in God. I know He is in control, and I know He has a plan for us. In spite of some of the bad stories I've shared in this book, I believe we are all destined for something. I believe we all have a purpose. I believe the outcome of those stories demonstrates that I was meant for something else. I'm not saying God helps you by sending negative experiences into your life. What I'm saying is that if that's not the story He has written for you, He will guide you to the right one. If the outcome of my negative story had been the alternative, I would've had a different life. I would've gone to jail for a long time. I would have had different experiences and lived a totally different lifestyle.

Two similar situations with similar results among others. I was sent home, not once but twice. How many people can say they've been arrested and charged with grand theft auto twice and sent home both time? As hard as that might be to understand and believe, but it is completely true. Either way, I cleaned myself up, I moved forward in a decent fashion. I made sure my companies helped lots of people. I have a great relationship with my wife, my sisters. I am raising two beautiful children. My relationship with them could not be better. They know Daddy is a little off now, but they're patient and understanding with me. I made sure I took full advantage of the opportunity. I am a man of

God. Without the spirit in your life, it really doesn't compute for me, how does life go on?

Back to business. Out of my three companies, only two survived. The permitting company didn't make it, since I myself did everything, and obviously I was not available. My labor company went dropped a lot in size, as did my DNA and drug testing company. Sadly, a lot of my clients thought I was going to die, so they moved on. Just to give you an idea, my labor company went from a 164 employees down to twenty at first. My DNA and drug testing went from four to just one. Life got a little harder. I kept the labor company going for a while, but unfortunately it became too much for me to manage. It went down to twenty employees and then to none. No more labor company. Financial problems, among others, became a huge factor. I had to give it up. Now at this specific moment, I only have one out of three. The DNA and drug testing company. The name had to change because of this mess also. I have always considered this to be my baby and now with time, I see why.

That's the only baby I have left. Its running consistently, keeping me busy enough and helping me support my family. Which I thank God for. No complaints. I went from having over 160 employees with all three companies to having only one at the current moment—me. Business is business, but I'm alive. I recently made sure to do one more thing that I should have done long ago and should definitely mention. I sat down and thought long and hard about Darling. I was thinking about this woman and how long we've been together and how much I've put her through. At this time we had been together eighteen years. This woman cleaned my butt while I was in a coma. If that doesn't spell love for you, I don't know what does? I knelt down and proposed once again, Only this time I made sure I followed through. We finally got married, twenty years after I asked her to be my girlfriend. I made Darling my wife. As for everything else, what can I tell you? I was reborn again, into a different life, maybe a little harder, but alive, with family, loved ones. And, of course, the man upstairs, God. With Him on my side, I'm ready for what comes next.

ADAPTING

I married my wife because I love her to death. I never really understood that saying. In this case, I would love her even after death if I could. Our love and relationship have definitely been tested. If you'd gone through what I've gone through, you wouldn't be the same. I'm not the same. Things that I didn't like before, I like them now. Things I would never have done before, I do them know. At least that's what I'm told. Because, again, I hardly have any recollection of my life before the accident. Darling and I had to get to know each other all over again. Or, rather, Darling had to get to know *me* again. The new me. I don't really notice it, but I imagine I'm a different person now. Thank God Darling is the awesome partner and woman she is. I imagine it hasn't been easy putting up with me. She's been an incredible woman over the years. She's an incredible mother and friend, and she's an incredible wife as well. I'm a lucky man to have her in my life. I have been extremely lucky to have her through all of this mess also. I love you, Darling!

My sisters have had to have a lot of patience with me while I've adapted to my new life. I've definitely given them some headaches while recuperating, but they've put up with me. All the women in my life have—my sister Yaritza, my younger sister, Denisse, and, of course, my new wife, Darling. Even my daughter, Zeani. I just want to say to you all, I'm sorry, I thank you immensely, and I love you more than words can express. I thank God I have you *all* in my life.

After the accident, for financial reasons among others, my immediate family had to move. Darling, Isaiah, Zeani, and I went to live with Denisse. We went from having a five-bedroom, four-bath home; a full-time, live-in maid; two cars; three motorcycles, to the four of us living in my little sister's guest room. Because I only had one out of three companies left, my income had gone down immensely. Darling had to go back to work. She was force to get a full-time job. Being the incredible woman she is, she's now the main financial support of our little family. I'm embarrassed to say this, since I've always been an independent man. I've worked so hard to be a good provider for my family and make sure my kids didn't go through the hard times we went through growing up with a single mother, but know I have no choice. I can't provide for my family as I always intended. Darling has stepped up and is keeping us above water. Thank you!

Remember my grandpa—the one that visited me while in coma? My family and I are living in his old home now. It's actually a mobile home, but we're all very comfortable here. My kids have got their own room, as do Darling and I. I thank God that I have my family close and that we're comfortable and healthy. I thank God every day that I'm here. I even catch myself praying when I'm driving. I'm definitely more grateful. I appreciate the little things a lot more.

Darling tells me that shortly before my accident, I stopped going to church because I was too busy with work. During what little time I had off, I wanted to be at home. Now, did I put God aside? Did I forget what was truly important? Well, with this lesson I've learned that we can never be too busy for God. His son was sacrificed for us. We can give up one hour a week to show our faith and dedication. I would like to teach and pass on that same lesson to my children. To be a better person, to believe, and to have faith because He is upstairs. To dedicate that time to Him. Meanwhile, I will remain focused. I will strive to be a better man for my family, a better brother to my sisters, a better family member. Period. I hope my recuperation comes to an end soon. I will move forward and continue to live my life with my chest out. I'm ready for whatever may come next.

Thank you *all* for reading my story. God bless!

I can be reached at:

Facebook: REBORNAT36 / PEDRO LEBRON

or

Rebornat36@gmail.com

CPSIA information can be obtained
at www.ICGtesting.com
Printed in the USA
LVHW021653110620
657586LV00002B/206

9 781630 503758